# ENCYCLOPEDIA BROWN'S
## Book of
# STRANGE BUT TRUE CRIMES

# ENCYCLOPEDIA BROWN'S
## Book of
# STRANGE BUT TRUE CRIMES

**Donald J. Sobol and Rose Sobol**

Illustrated by John Zielinski

**SCHOLASTIC
HARDCOVER**

Scholastic Inc.
New York

*Library of Congress Cataloging-in-Publication Data*

Sobol, Donald J., 1924–
    Encyclopedia Brown's book of strange but true crimes / Donald J.
Sobol and Rose Sobol.
        p.    cm.
    Summary: A collection of bizarre true stories about crimes,
criminals, prisoners, and police.
        1. Crime — Juvenile literature.    [1. Crime and criminals.
    2. Police.]    I. Sobol, Rose.    II. Title.
    HV6027.S63    1991
    364.1–dc20                                                  90-8617
                                                                  CIP
                            ISBN 0-590-44147-7                     AC
12 11 10 9 8 7 6 5 4 3 2 1                           1 2 3 4 5 6/9

                        Printed in the U.S.A.                      37
                First Scholastic printing, February 1991

For Donna,
who brightens our lives

All the stories in this book are true, though in many cases I have changed the name and/or the location.

— D.J.S.

# Contents

# ENCYCLOPEDIA BROWN'S
## Book of
# STRANGE BUT TRUE CRIMES

# The Case of the
# Two-Headed Toothbrush

"You know whom we haven't seen in weeks?" Encyclopedia Brown asked Sally Kimball, his junior partner in the Brown Detective Agency. "Melvin Pugh."

"I heard he's inventing a spray to make houseplants dance to a Strauss waltz," Sally said.

Melvin was always inventing something. Usually it was something nobody could use.

Two months ago, he had showed Encyclopedia his latest brainchild, a bowling ball without finger holes. It was for women who didn't want to ruin their nail polish.

"Melvin is a genius," Sally said. "He's just living on the wrong planet."

The two detectives were biking to the beach. As they turned down Fulver Street, Encyclopedia suddenly braked. "Hey, there's Melvin."

1

"And in trouble," Sally said.

Melvin stood on the sidewalk, surrounded by a gang of tough older boys who called themselves the Tigers. They should have called themselves the Mud Cards. They were always giving some small kid a dirty deal.

Bugs Meany, the Tigers' leader, wrinkled his nose at the sight of the two detectives. "Well, well, if it isn't the hotshot do-gooders," he taunted. "Make like Charles Lindbergh and take off."

"Encyclopedia!" Melvin cried. "Am I glad to see you! Bugs just stole my invention."

"Melvin better check his data base," Bugs growled. "The toothbrush is my invention."

Bugs held up two facing toothbrushes joined by a single handle. "With this little beauty, a person can brush the back and front of a tooth at the same time," he boasted. "It's the greatest gift to mankind since the cookie cutter with a trigger release."

"It's *my* invention, Encyclopedia," Melvin protested. "Bugs stole it from me while I was in the coin laundry down the street. Mom's washing machine broke. So I took the laundry out for her. I had the lid of the machine raised and was pushing the laundry down inside it with both hands when Bugs swiped the toothbrush from my back pocket."

"Man alive," Bugs moaned, smacking his forehead. "This kid is one heavy-duty liar! I had raised the lid on one of those machines and was pushing down my laundry with both hands. I was defenseless. So what happens? Melvin picks my back pocket and runs off with my two-headed toothbrush."

"Bugs Meany in a laundry?" Sally snapped. "Baloney! Since when do you wash anything?"

Bugs managed to keep his temper.

"My folks are away for the weekend," he said, winking at his Tigers. "I did my clothes in our washing machine. But our dryer is broken. So I came here to use a pay machine."

"Why didn't you hang your clothes on a line to dry?" Sally inquired.

"You peasant!" Bugs exclaimed. "Clothes hanging in the Meany backyard? Have you no refinement, no breeding?"

"Let's walk back to the coin laundry," Encyclopedia said. "I want to see your wet clothes, Bugs."

"Too late," Bugs said. "After Melvin stole my toothbrush, I had Spike Larson, my right-hand man, take the clothes to my house. That coin laundry isn't safe for honest citizens."

Encyclopedia nodded thoughtfully. Spike Larson wasn't in the group of Tigers.

"There has to be a witness," Sally said. "Someone in the laundry must have seen what happened."

"There weren't any other customers," Melvin muttered glumly.

"What about the person who runs the laundry?" Sally asked.

3

"As I came in, the phone rang and she went into the office to answer it," Melvin said. "The laundry was empty when Bugs stole my toothbrush."

"When you stole *my* toothbrush," Bugs insisted. "Now run along, Melvin, and invent something of your own. Wait, I've got it! Make it round and call it a wheel!"

The other Tigers howled with glee and joined in.

"Invent a shaving cream for boys under six. Have it smell like crayons."

"How about a stupid computer you can beat at checkers!"

"A self-cleaning bathtub!"

"Motorized garbage cans!"

"A swimming pool table!"

"Retread sneakers!"

At each suggestion, the Tigers rocked with laughter. Melvin looked ready to break into tears.

Sally shouted for the heckling to stop. Fists clenched, she marched up to Bugs. "I ought to knock the truth out of you, you pimplehead!"

Sally wasn't bluffing. She was the only kid in elementary school who dared to trade punches with the Tigers' leader. After taking one of her famous uppercuts, Bugs would wobble around like a drunk in an earthquake. Then he'd pitch to the ground and lie there till it was safe to get up.

"Back off," Bugs warned Sally. "I never went all out with you. But start something now, and I'll forget I'm a mother's dream. I'll fold you up like a pocketknife."

The other Tigers edged close to Sally.

Encyclopedia saw it was time to step in.

"You stole the two-headed toothbrush, Bugs," he said. "You've been lying."

"Oh, yeah?" Bugs retorted. "Prove it!"

"Allow me," Encyclopedia said politely.

He whispered into Bugs's ear.

Bugs blinked. Bugs reddened. Bugs looked as if he'd swallowed a bag of prunes.

"You know I was only fooling around," he mumbled weakly.

He handed Encyclopedia the toothbrush and tried to save face.

"Heck, I wouldn't want anyone thinking I really invented something this dumb," he jeered as he led his Tigers away.

Melvin hopped with joy. "The toothbrush will be bigger than my ladies' bowling ball. And I have you to thank, Encyclopedia. You ought to write a book."

"I'm collecting material," Encyclopedia said. "I've got a whole scrapbook filled with wacky true crimes."

"Let me see it!" Melvin begged.

"Come on over this evening," Encyclopedia invited.

The Browns had just finished dinner when Melvin rang the doorbell. Encyclopedia led him into the garage. From a shelf on the rear wall, the detective took down a large scrapbook.

"Here," he said to Melvin.

Melvin turned eagerly to the first page. He began to read. . . .

*For the solution to The Case of the Two-Headed Toothbrush, turn to page 113.*

# 1.
# Wacky Crimes

**"I don't."** Mauro Pirelli of Vicenza, Italy, was a jittery bridegroom.

Two hours before his wedding he had his hair cut. While seated in the barber's chair, he anxiously considered his future as a husband.

As his doubts worsened, inspiration struck.

He borrowed a car, sped to nearby Thiene, and climbed into a second-story window.

He clumped and clattered to make sure the home-owner heard him. Then he left a trail even a blind detective couldn't miss.

The police arrived in the nick of time — as Pirelli was going into the church to be married.

"I attempted a robbery just to get arrested and avoid the wedding," Pirelli confessed at his trial.

A panel of judges found him guilty of attempted robbery but withheld a prison sentence.

**He's alive and kicking, isn't he?**  The law finally caught up with Cristina Echvarria, a lady of many addresses. Among her offenses: practicing medicine without a license, and billing Medicaid for treating a 220-pound football player for diaper rash.

**It's the reel thing.**  A thief in Canton, China, suffered from catching a cola.

Yup, a cola, not a cold.

Guards at the Chrysanthemum Guest House nabbed him as he sipped a soda he had just reeled in.

Police identified him as the celebrated "fishing burglar." He specialized in pulling valuables through hotel windows with a fishing rod.

**The layered look.**   Two Senegalese crooks learned
clothes don't always make the man. Sometimes they
make the prisoner.

The pair broke into a clothing shop in Paris and
waddled out with lots of stylish threads. The cops
quickly spotted them. The two men were dressed
in a total of fourteen leather vests, three jackets,
one coat, and six pairs of trousers.

**Trial by file.**   For two years Astred Greene flew
the world free, saving herself an estimated $40,000
in air fares. She masqueraded as a flight attendant.

Greene got aboard overseas flights by walking past
the gate agent, who took her for a member of the crew.

One mistake did her in. She was too good at the job. Passengers wrote letters to the airline praising her helpfulness.

An office worker decided to start putting the letters in Greene's personnel file. Whoops, no file.

**Unforgettable 1.** "All I can remember about him is, he was stark naked," said Anne Barkley of Tampa, Florida, when asked to describe the man who stole her purse.

**Unforgettable 2.** "Well, he had big eyes," said Ellie Ford of Charleston, South Carolina, when asked to describe the Peeping Tom she saw at her window.

**Join the dinar's club.** In 1987, five tourists from West Germany were arrested for lighting their cigarettes with 100-dinar bills in the Koral Hotel in Umag, Yugoslavia.

One of the tourists took pictures of the lighting for laughs. A hotel employee became so angered that he called the police. The film was held for evidence.

A judge fined the tourists the equivalent of $30 each and denied them all "Yugoslav hospitality" (that is, the freedom to visit the country) for three years.

A 100-dinar note was worth about 15 cents.

**Cash and carry.**  Two women selected $419 worth of clothes in a department store in Heath, Ohio. They paid with a fake $1,000 bill.

The bill bore the phrases "A. Phony-bill" and "U. Cantcashit."

The store couldnotcashit. It was too large a bill. So a clerk took one of the women to a neighboring store.

No one there noticed anything unusual either, and the two women walked off with their new clothes and $581 in real-money change.

**All wet.**  Boyd Cross of Fort Lauderdale, Florida, came home from work to eat lunch and found a burglar in his bedroom.

Cross grabbed a gun, which he kept for protection. In the struggle with the burglar, the gun went off, wounding Cross's waterbed and flooding the house.

The burglar sprinted away with nothing except wet feet.

**Look away, look away.**  As part of a class project, three high school students got the okay from the manager of a Chicago department store to shoplift goods in full view of customers.

The students made out like bandits.

"They must have taken at least four hundred dollars' worth of merchandise," said their teacher.

During the three hours the students played their roles, there were more than 100 customers in the store. At least half saw the "shoplifting." The students got one dirty look. The rest of the customers either looked away or walked away.

"I'm totally amazed," their teacher said. "I thought maybe fifteen percent would report them. The indifference underscores what we're seeing more and more — a society that doesn't want to get involved."

**Hold 'em, roll.**   Mrs. Tillie Tangleber's restaurant in New York City served hard rolls. Hard as in *haarrrd.*

Early on a winter night Alexander Godwin, a barber, sat down at a table by the window facing the street. He ordered a cup of coffee and one of those hard rolls.

He had buttered the roll and was raising it to his mouth when things went crazy. A stranger stepped close to the window, whipped out a gun, and fired.

Godwin didn't have time to duck, and didn't have to. He had the roll.

The bullet splintered the window and struck the roll, which snuffed its force to a driblet. Deadened instead of deadly, the bullet dropped into Godwin's mouth, wounding him barely enough to draw blood.

The stranger apparently mistook Godwin for someone else and was never seen again.

**All are not hunters who blow the horn.** A Crime Stoppers TV program in Florida reenacted unsolved crimes with the hope that viewers who had information would tell the police.

*Realism* was the watchword. In one of the shows, a detective played the role of the robber of a milk store. A female rookie played his partner in crime.

Two weeks later a woman walked into police headquarters and surrendered. "You've got me redhanded," she said. She thought the reenactment of the holdup was a film taken while the actual crime was being committed.

**Kiss and wow!** Umberto Rizzo was a World War II airman when he kissed his sweetheart on a street corner in Messina, Sicily.

A policeman with no sense of romance reported his conduct.

Rizzo married the young woman, but it didn't help. He received a suspended three-month sentence for "indecency in a public place."

Forty years later the Italian Treasury Ministry decided that the sentence eliminated Rizzo, now 69, from a veterans' pension.

Moreover, the Ministry demanded back the $8,500 already paid him.

**Hidden assets.** In 1937, Joseph Mancini, a New York City druggist, saved $6,700 because he always wore long underwear, winter and summer.

Mancini had just sold his house for $68,000, and was carrying the $6,700 cash deposit. As he and his attorney entered a cab, two men shoved in behind them.

The attorney managed to jump as the cab slowed for a corner. The thieves jumped, too, with Mancini's pants.

Mancini told police that he had hidden the $6,700 in the leg of his underwear. The thieves got only the $15 in his pants.

**Know a woman by the companies she keeps.**
Dumbest Victims of the Year award for 1912 went
to the Hoboken, New Jersey, merchants who paid
a smartly dressed woman for goods she stole from
them.

Maisie B. Copeland was a wholesale shoplifter.
After a few days, she would return the merchandise
and coolly demand a refund in cash.

The merchants made good though they were
somewhat puzzled. She had no sales slips, and they
had no record of the sales.

Copeland swindled thousands of dollars before
store owners began swapping notes on a lady customer they never could satisfy.

She was taken to the Central Police Station,
where, like a lady of quality, she promptly swooned
to the floor.

**Sad but true.**   In 1930, the villagers of Zude, Poland, were convicted of stealing a forest.

The women did not appear in court, but the vil-
lage's 68 men did. They said they cut down the
nearby municipal forest to use as fuel. Otherwise,
they would have frozen during the winter.

The judge fined them and sentenced them to brief
terms in jail. He warned them not to steal any more
trees.

"Your honor," one villager replied. "That is impossible. I myself took home the last tree within miles and burned it."

**Time on his paws.**   A watch salesman in a shop in Shanxi, China, was being *watched* by police.

He had become the prime suspect when watches began disappearing left and right.

Just before police pounced, another salesman moved the watch counter.

Underneath was the real thief — a rat dwelling in a hole shining with 27 watches.

**It wooden work.**   Nevin Curtis had stopped for a red light in downtown Cincinnati, Ohio, when two thugs jerked open his car door. One of them seized him by the leg and tried to drag him out.

Curtis stomped on the gas and whizzed off. The shocked pair were left in a blast of exhaust — holding Curtis's artificial leg.

Although the leg cost Curtis $1,625, its resale value was small. It was made to his measure.

**'Hose guilty?**   Alfred Higgs of Portland, Oregon, said a nagging wife drove him to a life of crime.

After nine years of marriage, Higgs had had enough of her henpecking. He reached for a hose.

Oh, no, he didn't beat his wife. He unscrewed the nozzle and held up three stores at nozzlepoint.

"It was a spur of the moment thing," Higgs told

the judge. "I had been nagged so much by my wife about getting money, so I tried it."

**Bridge, anyone?** "Good thing the road is tied down," said a police spokesman after someone stole a 20-foot timber bridge that spanned a canal near Bunnell, Florida.

**Sleeper.** Two men with clubs forced their way into the apartment of Juan Sanchez.

Sanchez, who lived in a public housing project in Hato Rey, Puerto Rico, told the thieves he had nothing of any real value.

Unwilling to leave empty-handed, they took apart Sanchez's bed, loaded it on top of their car, and drove away.

**Can do.** Manfred Dreschler collected nickels, bottle by bottle and can by can.

He stole more than 60,000 empty, used bottles and cans from a warehouse in Geneva, New York. By turning them in at a redemption center, he collected the five-cent deposit on each and every one.

Investigators estimated that between 1980 and 1982 his piggy bank took in as much as $21,000. The sum represents about 400,000 bottles and cans.

**Doze weren't hepatitis shots.** A man who claimed to be a public health official telephoned the post office in Kaohsiung, Taiwan. He said a doctor was coming to vaccinate the employees against type-B hepatitis, a disease sweeping the area.

The "doctor" arrived in a hospital uniform. He told the seven employees that the shots might cause a brief spell of sleepiness. Hadn't they better close the post office for a few minutes?

The employees did as he advised and dozed off. When they woke up one and a half hours later, the "doctor" and all the cash — $5,526 — were gone.

**Sympathetic response.** An English hospital loaned teddy bears to small children during their stay. The stuffed animals made too big a hit. They were smuggled home at a rate of ten a month.

The nurses halted the practice by putting bandages on the bears. The children thought they were sick and needed to be kept in the hospital.

**Prime time.** Japanese police arrested Saburo Yoshida for making 1,400 long-distance telephone calls to Prime Minister Yasuhiro Nakasone's private office.

Yoshida called from a pay phone in Innoshima, 400 miles west of Tokyo, up to 100 times a day over a period of four months.

The calls lasted about three seconds because Yoshida could afford to deposit only one ten-yen (four cents) coin. He never spoke.

"My salary is low," explained Yoshida, a high school English teacher. "And I don't have any friends. Anyway, I thought I'd call the Prime Minister and annoy him."

**Skimming the cream.** Thieves pried off the lid of the safe in the Tinee Giant Market in Portsmouth, Virginia. The opening, alas, was too small for them to reach in and grab the money.

Their solution to the problem was all wet.

They dumped ten gallons of milk into the safe. The paper money floated within easy reach.

**You can't see the doctor without an appointment.** A burglar mistakenly sawed his way into Dr. Harley Kojak's office in Durham, North Carolina, and apologized in a note left on the doctor's desk.

"Sorry, wrong building, Doc."

Nothing, not even an aspirin, was missing.

**Stepping stones.** Harlan Orlando stole 175 diamonds worth $550,000 from a Nashville jewelry store. He hid them in a pair of old shoes, which he left with his father while he went on a fishing trip.

In his absence, his father gave some old clothing, including the shoes, to a child care center. The children played with the jewels for a week without knowing they were real.

Then Orlando appeared at the center. He demanded the jewels back so furiously that a teacher became suspicious. She called police.

Now, please, don't sit there mumbling, "If the shoe fits, wear it."

**He wasn't trying to stiff them.** Dr. Daniel Hunter was instructing a class of arthritis patients in Norfolk, Virginia.

One exercise called for the oldsters to raise their hands in the air.

"Stick 'em up!" Hunter hollered.

At that moment a passerby chanced to look through the window. Horrified, he telephoned the cops.

Police cars, sirens wailing, closed in on the building.

Hunter explained that the "stickup" was for the victims' health, not their money.

**Purse snatching — take two.** A pedestrian in Knoxville, Tennessee, saw a hoodlum snatch a woman's purse. He gave chase, tackled the crook, and held him for police — who arrived with surprising speed.

The problem was, the crook was a police officer. The purse-snatching was being staged for a local television station.

The crimestopper left the scene before anyone learned his name.

"I think he went away mad," said a police lieutenant. "I'd like to know who he was so we could write a letter praising him. He did exactly what I wish everyone would do."

**Hopping mad.** Someone got off on the wrong foot by stealing 300 sneakers from a shoe salesman's station wagon in Columbia, South Carolina.

There wasn't a matching pair of sneakers in the lot.

Shoe salesmen usually have signs on their cars stating:

> THESE SHOES ARE FOR ONE FOOT ONLY
> PLEASE DON'T STEAL

The robbed station wagon was signless.

**Expect to be treated as you treat others.** In a double take, Gilberto Mennes of Ponce, Puerto Rico, snatched the wallet of the mugger who had snatched his.

"It was sticking out of his back pocket," said Mennes. "I didn't have time to think. I just grabbed it. He never looked back."

Mennes's wallet contained only identification papers.

The mugger's wallet had a driver's license and $33, which he got back after his arrest.

**It might have been worse.** Three thieves took almost everything valuable from 50 guests at a wedding party in Bergamo, Italy. The softies let the bride keep her wedding ring.

**He struck oil.** After two flags were stolen from the post office in Oshkosh, Wisconsin, the postmaster had the 20-foot pole greased. The Stars and Stripes went up and down, but not the thief.

**One for the books.** Police searching the home of a Wisconsin man found more than 4,000 public library books "borrowed" over the past 20 years.

**And the dog's name is Buck.** A visitor to Davenport, Iowa, told police that he had been robbed of $300 by a "big, friendly dog" obviously trained to lift wallets.

**What a gas.** A robber hit a Tulsa service station eight times in the same year. Practice made him close to perfect. He shaved his holdup time to 30 seconds.

**All that glitters is not gold.** The old proverb was learned afresh by a gang of thieves who robbed the Tse Sui Luen Jewelry Store in Hong Kong.

The nine gold bars they stole from a show window

were fake, worth about $800 instead of the expected $108,000.

The disgusted gang dumped the bars in a restaurant men's room along with a note addressed to the jewelry store manager. The note bitterly complained that he was cheating his customers.

The manager denied the charge. "It is normal practice to display fake gold bars in the store's windows for safety reasons," he said.

The thieves did get away with $42,000 in jewelry.

**Birdbrain!** Acting on a tip, Dallas police found hundreds of dollars' worth of stolen merchandise in the lodging of a 19-year-old youth on probation.

A parrot in the room greeted the officers with "Hello, Cindy. Hello, Jack." The youth insisted he'd bought the bird from a man known to him only as Shorty.

Police checked through reports of stolen parrots. They found that a parrot named Jack, valued at $2,800, had been stolen from Cindy Mathesson, owner of a card shop.

Mathesson was summoned to the police station. At the sight of her, the parrot flapped its wings excitedly and screaked, "Cindy!"

"Jack!" she cried back.

The youth pleaded guilty to theft and was sentenced to three years in prison.

"The moral of this story," said an assistant district attorney, "is that if you steal a talking parrot, you'd better retrain him."

**Soap story.** Trudy Case of Walla Walla, Washington, came home to find her front door forced open.

The only thing the intruder had taken was a bath.

"Maybe we'll have to round up housebreakers who normally are dirty and now are suddenly clean," remarked a police officer.

**One for the road.** On a Monday morning Allen Statler opened his auto repair shop in Des Moines and thought something looked different. Over the weekend, thieves had hauled away 25 feet of sidewalk in front of his business, brick by brick.

**Seventy-six would be the spirit.** Skateboarder Mitch Collins, 19, was pulled over for speeding on the downhill of a California interstate highway and told he was doing 72 miles an hour.

"That simply isn't true," said Collins. "I was doing seventy-five!"

**He had it maid.** An unidentified "victim" in Gilroy, California, returned home to find it had been cleaned out.

Correction: cleaned *up*.

Someone had gathered the dirty laundry, made

the bed, washed the dishes, and hung new drapes. The volunteer housekeeper left a note:

> Dear Sir,
> I hope you don't mind. I cleaned your house. Don't worry. I didn't take anything because my father is a Duke in Spain. I'll clean your house for as long as you live here.
>
> Prince Eddie.

"We're not sure what we could charge him with," said the local police commander. "It's too bad he didn't break into my house."

**Overtime.** How many employees break into a business to go to work?

The owner of a fast-food restaurant in Memphis declared bankruptcy. That night he had all the locks on the building changed.

The next morning four employees showed up at the regular opening time. They smashed the drive-in window, crawled inside, got the deep fryer and the soda machine going, and began serving takeout orders.

It was business as usual — until the owner drove by.

The foursome had pocketed $398 before the police shut them down.

**Purse snacker.** Officials at a zoo in Arnhem, Holland, put up signs warning visitors to guard their handbags.

Not only did the thief make the zoo her home, she had a marvelously long reach, and she was beyond the law.

Her name was Quimba. She was rather attractive if you like them big. However, she wasn't the type heroes chase after.

An elephant, Quimba used her trunk to pluck the handbags, which she swallowed with a satisfied *glub*.

**Paper chase.**   Thieves hit a stationery company in Coventry, England, seven times in less than a year and walked off with everything they could lift.

As if figuring it would be an even easier place to loot without a security system, they sneaked back and stole the burglar alarm.

"They probably needed the alarm to protect the eighteen thousand dollars' worth of stuff they stole from us," said a company spokesman.

**Thanks, we needed that.**   Fifteen Democratic committeemen were gathered in Denver to assign subjects for the state platform in the November election.

"Who's going to take crime?" asked the chairman of the resolutions committee. No one answered.

He repeated the question twice, but got no takers.

Finally he said, "Someone has to take crime."

At that, three men charged into the room, took everyone's money, and charged out.

**It's not what you say, it's how you say it.**   In Rochester, New York, Janice Manton was seen leaving a jewelry store holdup where nine rings had been stolen at gunpoint.

She was overtaken driving to Henrietta. Police searched the car, uncovered a gun, but no rings. They tried to question her.

She replied by pressing her lips together.

Finally, she mumbled that she wanted to see her lawyer.

Mumbling was her goof.

Police found the nine rings in her mouth.

**Desert raiders.** In Arizona cactus rustling became so common that the plant had to be protected by law.

Yet the thievery continues. In one case, a 19-foot saguaro cactus was stolen in Quartzite. Wanted posters of the plant were nailed up along the state border.

A tipster spotted the cactus on sale in a Nevada nursery for $15,000. The elderly couple from whom

it was stolen picked it out of a police lineup. The
thieves were then caught and convicted.

**Try it, you'll like it.**   A gang in India had thievery
down to a tea.

The gang mingled with regular tea sellers on the
platform of the Kalyan railroad station and sold passengers tea laced with knockout drops.

As the train pulled out, members of the gang
climbed aboard. As soon as their victims fell asleep,
they relieved them of their cash and valuables and
hopped off at the next stop.

**Bedside manner.**   An undertaker in Kuala Lam-
pur, Malaysia, was fined the equivalent of $12 for
entering a hospital without permission and selling
coffins to the patients.

# 2.
# Dumbo Desperados

**No way out.** In Coventry, England, a clothing store burglar seeking a fast getaway went bananas running into one fake exit after another. All led to a brick wall.

After trying 12 dummy doors, which were background scenery for a fashion display, he climbed a staircase, lost his footing, and knocked himself out.

**Doughnut unto others.** In Frankfort, Kentucky, a Brinks guard carried a bag of money from a supermarket and put it in his armored truck. Feeling hunger pangs, he went back and bought a bag of doughnuts.

As he approached his truck, two armed thugs knocked him down. The birdbrains grabbed the bag of doughnuts and, believing themselves rich, escaped by car.

**Money to burn.**   A gang of safecrackers called itself the Japanese Ninja, after the Japanese assassins of feudal days.

The Ninjas operated in California in the 1980s with burning failure. In three robberies in a row, they used blowtorches to open safes, frying to ashes the money inside.

**Role playing.**   Time caught up with a pair of house burglars in São Paulo, Brazil.

They were so old that one burglar, Pedro de

Rosas, 74, couldn't hear his partner, Juan Alves, 73, scream that the police were coming.

"They should have known better," said police inspector Osvaldo da Silva. "I think they wanted to relive the good old days. But Alves, who doesn't hear well, was still busy stealing when we arrived."

De Rosas made an effort to run for it, but his varicose veins held him to a fast shuffle.

**Photo finish.** It wasn't so much the crudeness of the phony bank notes that irked the judge in Nairobi, Kenya. It was the picture.

The counterfeiter, Whythe Ngugi, said he saw nothing wrong with printing his own picture on the 100-shilling note, worth $7.70. His bearded portrait replaced that of President Moi in the center of the bill.

The self-centered Ngugi pondered the high price of vanity behind bars.

**Doesn't everyone save receipts?** Harry Lyle picked up a hitchhiker outside Bismarck, North Dakota. The hitchhiker drew a gun, took $60 from Lyle, and asked for a *receipt*. When the police tracked him down, he still had the receipt in his pocket.

**That's the way the ice floes.** On a freezing day in January, three girls, all 16 years old, mugged a woman on the northern tip of Manhattan Island.

They took her purse and chose a tricky escape route along the ice-clogged shore.

All at once they found themselves drifting away on a hunk of ice about six feet square. They floated north on the Hudson River for an hour until rescued by a police helicopter.

"They didn't say much of anything," said the pilot, Robert Hegel. "They were glad to get off even if it meant getting locked up."

**Are you sure Houdini started this way?** A 16-year-old in New Haven, Connecticut, attempted to force his way into a house and became stuck in the window grating.

He had removed two bolts from the bars around

a first-floor window and had started crawling through. One of the bars snapped back and trapped him. Halfway in and halfway out, he managed to reach the telephone and called 911, the emergency number. He asked if someone would please come and rescue him.

As he was led away by the police, he muttered, "I'm embarrassed. This is my first burglary."

**Weight-watchers.** Food was steadily disappearing from a warehouse in Prague, Czechoslovakia. After $120,000 worth of munchies had vanished, suspicion centered on the warehouse supervisor. He had ballooned to 506 pounds.

The judge put him on a 12-year diet of prison chow.

**High flier.** Cat burglar Garvey Forman plied his craft at a theatrical boardinghouse in Chicago. In the course of his search for goodies, he tiptoed into the room of a sturdy six-footer, Mrs. Beatrice Renn.

Renn shrilled the alarm and applied a numbing headlock. With the last of his strength, Forman wrenched free and wobbled into the hall. He was greeted by members of a circus troupe.

Hyman Reinke, the strongman, seized him and caused him to perform a brilliant series of contortions. Others joined in the fun.

Forman escaped by accomplishing a passable version of a big-top act, the "flying leap for life," down a flight of stairs. Pursued by the circus troupe, he dashed along Halsted Street and flung himself into the safety of a policeman's arms.

**They threw the book at them.** In Camden, New Jersey, a couple had a gun, but Bonnie and Clyde they weren't.

They tried to hold up a *library.*

An assistant librarian convinced them the library had only a few coins in overdue book fines.

"Looks like we picked the wrong place to rob," the woman grumped to her companion.

Thirty minutes later they were arrested reading magazines in front of the library.

**Long shot.** A gambler from Dayton, Ohio, waltzed blithely up to the cashier's window at a Las Vegas casino and asked for $7,500 in chips.

The cashier immediately became suspicious. The gambler's cash was in bank wrappers and stuffed in a bank bag.

The gambler lost his stake — the loot from a bank holdup — before he could make a bet.

**Okay, okay, how about a pretzel?** A masked man waved a kitchen knife at a clerk in a liquor store in Jackson, Mississippi, and angrily demanded money.

The clerk responded by smacking a metal pipe on the counter.

Shaken, the masked man blurted, "Just give me twenty dollars."

The clerk glared silently.

"Can I take a bag of potato chips?"

When the clerk shook his head, the masked man skedaddled.

**Bad training.** A motorman in New York City stopped his subway train and took $11 from a drunk sleeping on a platform. He chose the wrong victim. The drunk was a police decoy.

**Name brand.** Sheila Townsend of Duluth, Minnesota, pleaded not guilty to breaking into a car and stealing clothing and other property. The attire she wore to court, a sports warm-up outfit, said otherwise.

"Those are my clothes!" gasped the victim, Mrs. Ida Kearns. "My name is inside."

It sure was, on the collar. Townsend changed her plea to guilty.

**A mansion is a *big* house.** A midnight burglar slipped through the window of a mansion in Scarsdale, New York, and became lost. He did find a bedroom, shook owner Jason Frankenthal awake, and asked the way out.

Frankenthal ushered him to the front door. Then he described the confused burglar to the police, who made the arrest before dawn.

**Help needed — and how.**  Two harebrained hoods entered a U-Totem convenience store in Cleveland and requested job application forms.

They filled out the forms, left the store, and returned with a gun.

They didn't get much opportunity to spend their $380 take. The boneheads had left their job applications forms, filled out with their names and addresses, in the store.

**Catchy little number:**  A young man tried to telephone his father in Shreveport after breaking into a city building in New Orelans.

Instead of dialing "9" to make an outside call, his finger slipped and he dialed "0." That connected him with police dispatchers. He was still holding the telephone when officers came for him.

**He shot the works.**  Tony Mercir broke into a city building in Pittsburgh. He found a Polaroid camera in one of the offices and took his own picture. When it came out black, he tossed it into a trash basket.

"He didn't understand how the camera works," said one officer. "It takes a little time for the picture to develop."

37

Now think hard. When was the last time you saw a thief take his own picture at the scene of the crime and leave it there?

Armed with a copy of the photo, a police officer spotted Mercir, a picture of innocence, in downtown Pittsburgh. He was snapped again — with handcuffs.

**True grit.** In Philadelphia, Janice Fullwood, a barmaid, had a splitting headache. A thug made it worse. He put a pistol to her temple.

"Open the cash register and pass me the money," he ordered.

Instead of jumping to obey, she snapped, "I'm sick. Get it yourself."

The gunman hesitated, looked around, and decided to leave.

"I wasn't scared," said Fullwood. "I was just sick, and I wasn't moving for anybody."

**How's buy you?** Two teenagers stopped at a rare coin and stamp gallery in Montgomery, Alabama. They had some 17th-century coins to sell.

Owner Mason Stadler recognized the coins, which he kept in his home. He also noticed one of the youths was wearing his niece's gold charm bracelet and his wife's necklaces.

Mason told the teenagers to have a seat. His 230-

pound, 6-foot-3-inch security guard kept his eye on the thieves until police arrived.

The coins and jewelry had been stolen from Stadler's home three hours earlier, along with a shotgun, a battery-operated television, and a portable radio.

"Of all the houses in the city to burglarize," said Sergeant Bill Atwater, "they break into his house and turn around and try to sell the stuff back to him. They were dumbfounded that this could possibly happen. They couldn't believe it."

**Clean living.** Stockholm, Sweden, had a "wash-and-wear" thief. He would shed his dirty duds, bathe, and put on the clothes of the homeowner, before slipping out with guns, cameras, and jewelry. He flubbed, finally. He left his name and address in the clothes he tossed to the floor.

**Underwhere?** Sean Starr pleaded guilty to shoplifting in a pet shop in northern England. An employee grew suspicious of his odd walk as he headed for the door. Police found a pair of four-foot pythons stuffed in his underwear.

**Which way to the recruiting office, sergeant?** Three bumbling bandits invaded a house they thought belonged to a drug dealer in Miami, Florida.

It didn't. It belonged to a fireman, Louis Johnson, and his wife, Barbara.

Two of the bandits, Ed Mullins and Arthur Lopes, tied up the couple. The third, Alfred Fowler, held a gun on the Johnsons to show he meant business. The bullets fell out.

Next they snipped the cord of a can opener, thinking it was a telephone line, and ransacked the house.

The only drugs they found were pills Johnson took for a heart condition. They settled for cash, jewelry, liquor, and clothing. The most valuable item, Mrs. Johnson's ring, they dropped in the garage as they raced for their car.

The best was saved for last.

Speeding away, the champs overshot their turn, thought a guardhouse was a tollbooth, and whizzed into the Homestead Air Force base.

The military police let them call a lawyer.

**You're only as good as your tools.** A man stood at the counter of a convenience store in Lansing, Michigan, and asked for a pack of cigarettes. He reached into his pocket as if reaching for money and produced a revolver.

"Don't move!" he bawled.

Whereupon something did — the barrel of his gun. It fell off.

"Never mind," he said to the clerk, picked up the barrel, and beat a hasty retreat.

**Sorry, the number you have reached is in working order.** An anonymous caller made Dan Barkley an offer he couldn't refuse.

The caller had stolen jewelry, rings, and diamonds to sell. But he had dialed the wrong number. Oh, boy, did he ever! Barkley was a New York City police captain.

**Don't get around much anymore.** Steven Corey of Detroit taped a shotgun to his leg. While walking toward a drugstore he was planning to rob, he shot and wounded himself.

**Short fuse, long walk.** If you're going to be a robber, it doesn't pay to lose your temper.

In St. Louis a man drove up to a gas station, approached the attendant, and demanded money. The attendant told him all the cash was locked up in a safe.

The would-be robber stomped off in a rage, forgetting his car.

The next morning came the reminder. License plate numbers aren't fingerprints, but tag you they can.

**Leave the driving to us.** Six months after jumping bail on a disorderly conduct charge in central New York, Charles Hanson was hitchhiking to New York City. A car with two men stopped for him. As he

41

climbed into the backseat, one of the men turned around and said, "Charlie, you're under arrest again."

The man was the officer who had made the original arrest.

**Bud wiser.** "After the mistakes I've made, I don't think I have any political future whatsoever." The speaker, a 20-year-old freshman state senator, had just been convicted of stealing two cases of beer from a food store.

**Good-bye, two shoes.** Paul Caruso broke into a home in Mt. Kisco, New York. He took off his sneakers and stuffed his wallet with his birth certificate and a picture of himself (wearing the sneakers) into a sneaker. Surprised by the homeowner, Caruso fled, leaving behind the sneakers and wallet. He did ten years without them.

**Slick trick.** Two dumbdumbs bought a can of motor oil in a convenience store in Davie, Florida. They put the can into a paper bag.

Then they held up the clerk and put the cash into a second paper bag.

Grinning with success, they hustled out with one of the bags — the one with the motor oil.

"Why in the world these guys were not able to keep straight which bag the money was in is beyond me," said a detective. "But then, we're not dealing with brain surgeons."

**Party crashers.**   A West German youth passed stolen goods out the window of a house in Frankfurt and straight into the hands of police.

The police had come to the scene to investigate a suspicious noise. At the sight of the law, the youth's two good buddies fled.

"Here . . . take this cassette player," the young burglar said. "Now give me the crowbar. There's a lot more."

The police cooperated until they had collected all the evidence they needed.

**Say jeez!** In Rome, Italy, a couple of hoodlums riding motorscooters forced themselves into the picture. Two women tourists from Japan were posing for a friend when the hoodlums roared up, bowled them over, and roared off with their jewelry and purses.

The friend kept clicking his camera. Police used the mug shots to make the arrest.

**Shop at home.** A burglar looting the home of Murray Resnick of Savannah was surprised in the act. Waving a handgun, he herded Resnick, his wife, and three children into a bedroom.

Resnick stayed cool. He admired the burglar's gun and offered to buy it.

The burglar said he wanted $40 and not a penny less.

Resnick wrote out a personal check to cash. The burglar grabbed it, handed over the gun, and raced away.

**Nickled and dimed.** Back in 1915, some fast-working burglars moved a heavy safe from its position under an electric light in the Woolworth five-and-dime store in Camden, New Jersey. In its place they substituted a safe made of cardboard. The crudely constructed mock-up was good enough to fool the night watchman on his rounds.

The burglars had pushed the store's "burglar-proof" safe into a dark corner. After the watchman passed, they forced the door open. The only hitch in the operation was the money inside, less than $100.

**Bag man.** Albert McDennis of New York City was walking his dog. Abiding by the city's cleanup law, he had carefully put the waste into a paper bag when a burly man came up and snarled, "Give me what you got there."

McDennis handed over the bag without delay.

Said McDennis, "He must be New York's dumbest mugger."

**What a pill.** The burglar had a bad case of nerves. He kept threatening Cara Phillips as he ransacked her St. Paul home.

The strain took its toll. He complained of head pains and asked for some aspirin.

Phillips handed him Valium tablets from her bedside table. He gulped them down.

When he was slumbering like a bear, she telephoned police.

**Don't call us, we'll call you.** Three dimwits in Peterborough, England, kidnapped Federigo Dante, an Italian baker.

They telephoned his home and demanded $7,500 in ransom. A family member asked for more time to raise the money.

The kidnappers agreed to the delay.

"We won't call again," one of them said. "When you have the money, ring us."

He helpfully supplied a telephone number.

Guess what happened next.

**Ask a foolish question.** A gent with zero brainpower asked a policeman in Athens, Georgia, to find out if he was wanted anywhere.

A computer answered that he was — for a holdup in his hometown of Tuckahoe, New York, two years before.

The FBI brought him home.

**It's getting harder to make a dishonest buck.** In Little Rock, Arkansas, a dingbat entered a jewelry store and took the routine out of the clerk's day.

"This is a stickup," he announced.

He fumbled through his pockets, frowned, and grumbled, "I forgot my gun. I'll be right back."

When he returned a few minutes later, the clerk said she didn't have the money ready for him.

She did have a cop.

**Now *that's* acting.** An unemployed actor attempted to hold up a San Diego restaurant with a hairbrush and was convicted of armed assault.

# 3.
# Honest to Goodness

**Capitol idea.** A small glass paperweight was sent to Governor Anthony S. Earl of Wisconsin 20 years after it had been snitched.

A woman confessed that her son had taken it during a class visit to the capitol.

She wrote the governor:

> *I've always thought we should send it back where it belonged, but we never did until this morning. Please forgive my son for taking it, and also me for not insisting that he send it right back.*

**Welcome to the fold.** A man in his 80's rang Mason Haines's doorbell in Louisville, Kentucky.

The elderly stranger offered to return Haines's wallet. But first Haines had to sign a note promising not to have him arrested.

"I signed but couldn't believe what was happening," Haines said. "He wouldn't permit any questions and gave no explanation. He just took the paper and left."

The wallet had vanished, had been mislaid or was lifted, 40 years ago. Everything was there — cash, Social Security card, draft registration, and family pictures.

**The light touch.** After stringing up her Christmas lights, Betsy Hoffa of Phoenix, Arizona, laid a note on her porch for the thieves who had ripped off her two dozen bulbs the previous year.

The note read:

> *I think that having all the lights stolen last year was enough. There are children living here who would like to enjoy Christmas. We're trying to celebrate the birth of our Savior, not thieves.*

The following night she found the stolen bulbs on her doorstep along with a note written in a child's script:

> *We're sorry, we were only borrowing the lights. We replaced the broken one. Merry Christmas to you and your kids.*

Commented Mrs. Hoffa, "Thank goodness for honest thieves."

**An old clipping.** "Are you Eddie?" a gray-haired man said anxiously to Eddie Fenton, owner of a barbershop in Chicago.

Fenton, busy with a customer, nodded.

The man laid an envelope on the counter and said, "This is yours." On his way out, he added, "I'll be back for a haircut."

In the envelope was $125 stolen from Fenton 17 years before.

**Boo!** The week before Halloween, Sandy Halotte of Concord, New Hampshire, heard a noise on her porch during the night. The next morning her two daughters, aged 5 and 8, tearfully reported their pumpkin was gone.

For a day the thief apparently tussled with the memory of how he had felt when *his* pumpkin was stolen. The memory won.

He returned the Halottes' pumpkin with the note:

*Sorry, I forgot. It happened to me when I was 3, and I cried my brains out. I'm really sorry.*

                               *The Night Man.*

**Don't knock on this wood.** A Canadian tourist mailed back a sliver of wood he had filched as a souvenir from the *Wasa*, a 17th-century ship being restored in Stockholm, Sweden.

The thief said his luck had soured since the theft. In a letter to the restorers, he related his woes:

*I am normally not superstitious, but since I stole that little piece of wood from the ship I have been hit by bad luck, diseases, and disappointments. I had made it hardly 50 yards from the entrance of the* Wasa *Shipyard when I discovered that a jar of syrup in my bag had broken. I have also been plagued by severe pain in my back and been betrayed in love and friendship. I hope that by returning it I will regain my good luck.*

                         *A Guilty Canadian.*

*Wasa* was, in fact, a jinxed ship. Starting on her maiden voyage in 1628 as the king's flagship, she didn't make it out of Stockholm harbor. Horrified onlookers watched her capsize and sink. She was raised in 1961 after lying on the sea floor for 333 years.

**Cross my heart.**   A mugger with a fast tongue and slow wits promised to repay the two Jersey City women whom he robbed of $101.

To prove his good faith, he gave the women his name and address in Bangor, Maine.

A week later he still insisted he would pay back the $101.

"A promise is a promise," he said from his cell in the county jail.

**Gone but not forgotten.**   Someone stole the gumball machine from Jerry Pinter's coin laundry in Burlington, Wisconsin. Twenty-two years later, Pinter got a call from the thief, who wanted to make amends.

"I thought it was somebody trying to give me the business," said Pinter. "I couldn't believe it."

The caller asked the value of the machine in 1968, the year it was stolen. Pinter checked around and settled on $25.

The thief sent $118, saying in an unsigned letter that there was about $32 worth of gum and coins in the machine he stole. The rest was conscience money.

**Better late . . .** In 1982, ten dollars arrived at Loeb's Department Store in Lafayette, Indiana. The money was in a plain white envelope, along with a letter:

> *In the early 1930s I owed Loebs I think eighty-seven cents and never paid it. Occasionally thru the yrs, I think of the wrong I done, so am sending you ten dollars. Hope this will take care of interest and all. Hope you will forgive me. Thank you.*

The letter was without a signature, but the somewhat shaky handwriting was clearly a woman's.

"Nowadays, the store wouldn't even send out a bill for eighty-seven cents," said the store manager. "It wouldn't be worth it. For five dollars we probably wouldn't send one out. Back in the thirties, however, you could buy a towel for eighty-five cents or a pair of hose for fifty cents. That was the heart of the Depression, and whatever she bought probably meant a great deal to that woman at that time. It's quite possible she just didn't have the money to pay it off. When I think of the guilt trip she's had for more than fifty years. . . ."

**Ring out the old.**   A pine tree belonging to Parker Everns of Chippewa, Wisconsin, was chopped down and carried off three days before Christmas.

Six weeks later the less-than-sorry thief returned it in a plastic bag with a note attached:

> *Dear Sir,*
> *Thanks for the use of the tree. It really made our Christmas. I wish you could have seen how we had it decorated up. I was looking at all the other trees in your yard and, with a little trimming on your part, one of them could qualify for our tree next Christmas. Thanks again. See you next year!*

**You can say that again.**  A young man robbed a Cumberland Farms store in Manchester, New Hampshire. The next day he stuck his head in the door and told the clerk he was sorry.

Did he give back the money?

"He wasn't that sorry," said the clerk.

**Change of heart.**  The Phoenix office of the FBI received a cardboard box filled with $36,000 in $100 bills. The sender explained in an unsigned note that the money was from a bank robbery in Gallup, New Mexico, plus interest. Two months earlier, a single gunman had bound and gagged the tellers in the Western Bank in Gallup and cleaned out the cash drawers.

**And they always assumed it was a tree swallow.**  A guilt-ridden tourist who picked an orange from a grove in Santa Ana, California, mailed an apology and a one-dollar bill to the sheriff's department.

The note read:

> *I want to pay for the orange I picked along the highway in Orange County. I had this feeling that I must be in heaven with all these oranges growing, and I must have one. I am sorry. Please pass this on to some orange grower.*

**The foot's on the other shoe.** "I wouldn't be doing this but my kids are starving," a masked gunman said after robbing a shoe store in Cedar Rapids, Iowa. He gave the two clerks $20 each.

# 4.
# You Can Bank on It

**Safe and sorry.** Safecrackers tried to blow open a safe in the Provinsbanken in Munkebo, Denmark. The safe survived, but the bank collapsed.

**A lot of us know the feeling.** A month after holding up a bank near Evanston, Illinois, the culprit came back and scolded the teller.

"You gave me too many one-dollar bills last time," he complained. "I don't want that many ones. Do it right this time."

**Things are seldom what they seem.** In Detroit, a bank robbery suspect being pursued by two armed guards dodged into what he thought was an apartment building. He wound up behind bars in nothing flat. The "apartment building" was a police station.

**Run for the money.** Joseph Clemmer leaped over the counter of a bank in Lincoln, Nebraska, socked the teller, and gathered up $645.

So far, so good.

The problem started when Clemmer ran. Bank employees and customers ran, too. After him.

He threw some money at them. They just ran faster.

"Are you crazy?" he screamed. "Take the money!"

He jumped into a taxi. His pursuers pounded on the windows and shouted, "He's a thief!"

Pushing out the other side, he dropped more money and sprinted off. He got about 50 feet and was mobbed.

Police tied him to 20 holdups in the previous two months.

Now if he'd thrown banana skins . . .

**Since you put it that way.** Kevin Otis of Glasgow, Scotland, had his heart set on becoming a bank robber, and he didn't care who knew it.

He pushed to the front of the line, but a bank official told him to wait his turn.

After a fidgety ten minutes, his big moment arrived. He stepped up to the teller and recited his piece: "Quick, all your money!"

Instantly an alarm rang. Otis scrammed, but was caught.

At the police lineup, the bank official was unable to identify him.

"Hey, what's the matter with you?" Otis shrieked. "Don't you recognize me?"

That was enough for the police.

**Faint-hearted.** A shortage of nerve did in a dumbo who tried to hold up a bank in Spokane, Washington. Shaking all over, he pointed a toy gun at Winifred Owens, a teller, and stammered for her money.

When she said she didn't have any, he stopped shaking and fainted dead away.

Police found his getaway car parked near the bank. The doors were locked and the keys were inside.

**Better watch out.** Worst performance by a singing Santa Claus occurred in Shreveport, Louisiana. A Santa in sunglasses relieved a bank there of $1,000 while softly croaking, "We wish you a merry Christmas, we wish you a merry Christmas."

**Against all odds.** Two hoodlums with more luck than brains pulled a bank job and got away, despite themselves.

Wearing ski masks and dark blue jumpsuits, they cleaned out the teller drawers and a cash machine of a bank in Vancouver, British Columbia.

Once outside, they fastened shut the front doors of the bank with a heavy chain and padlock. That

was supposed to keep everyone inside for a while —
unless, of course, someone used the back door.

Determined not to be caught, the twosome coolly
followed their carefully thought-out plan. They
dropped boards spiked with nails in the parking lot.
The nails pointed sharp end up to puncture the tires
of vehicles giving chase.

Yep, you guessed right.

They ran over a board with their stolen getaway
car. A flat tire stopped them a block and half from
the bank.

When last seen, they were legging it across a field
with the bank's money.

**Cheers.**   After robbing a bank in Toronto, Canada,
of $3,000, a thirsty gunman strolled down the street
and into the corner tavern.

He bought drinks for everyone.

He was sitting at the bar with his new friends and
the bag of money in front of him when police arrived.

**Sacked for a loss.**   A fast-thinking teller in Columbia, South Carolina, foiled a robber with a question.

She read his note. *This is a stickup. I want all
your money.* Flipping over the note, she wrote on
the back, *Have you anything to put it in?*

The man read the question, shook his head rue-
fully, and high-tailed it for the door.

**Wrong-way robber.** A bearded gent pushed six $50 bills at a teller in Federal Savings and Loan in Akron and asked for three $100 bills.

As she began to peel off the bills, he fumbled on a ski mask and lowered a hand into his pocket as if reaching for a gun.

The teller promptly dropped out of sight behind the counter. The bearded man froze in dismay.

Then, completely rattled, he fled empty-handed, leaving behind the bank's money and his own six $50 bills.

**Mask, and ye shall receive.** In Yakima, Washington, many people wore paper masks to protect themselves from volcanic ash after Mount St. Helens erupted. A bank there posted a sign:

FOR SECURITY REASONS
PLEASE REMOVE MASKS BEFORE ENTERING

**A little knowledge is a dangerous thing.** A couple of armed chumps swept into what they thought was a bank in Montgomery, Alabama.

After madly pulling open drawers in the search for cash, they finally heeded what the employees were saying. It wasn't a bank anymore.

The dopey duo had stormed an accounting firm, which had occupied the premises for more than a month.

**A novel approach.** With the arrest of Mike Rodin in Dallas, the FBI at last had the bank robber famed for his lengthy holdup notes.

"Most notes say, *This is a stickup,* and ask for money," said an FBI agent. "This guy writes you a nice letter and then goes from there."

Sometimes it took bank tellers several minutes just to read Rodin's notes and figure out what he wanted.

**No inventory.** The demand was classic: "Give me all your money."

The response wasn't. The teller told the holdup man that the bank had no money.

No joke.

The bank, the Mellon Boulder Industrial Bank in Boulder, Colorado, had voluntarily liquidated its assets and had quit accepting deposits.

**Decisions, decisions.** The man had sat in his car for more than an hour in front of the Timewell State Bank in Timewell, Illinois. Finally the bank's president went outside and asked if he could be of help.

"Well, I'm not going to do it, but I've been debating whether or not to rob this bank," the man told him, and drove away.

**Hi, remember me?** "I just wanted to see if she'd recognize me," Allister Fallowfield told the police.

Two days after robbing a bank near London, Fallowfield had returned and inquired of the same teller about opening a savings account.

She recognized him.

**Stalled.** Despite having just heisted $13,492 from a bank in Portland, Oregon, Eddie Severen couldn't find change for a pay toilet in a nearby coin laundry. He didn't even have a one-dollar bill to feed the change maker.

He was flipping desperately through a wad of bills when a bank guard collared him.

**Check point.** Eunice Dunlop, a bank teller in Dundee, Scotland, had her checkbook stolen when her car was burglarized. The following month a customer gave her a check to cash.

"I thought," said Dunlop, "this is my check and it isn't my handwriting. Then it hit me — that's my check and it's stolen. I literally was ready to go over the counter after the guy."

Police saved her the trouble.

**What a line.** John Trent of Liverpool, England, had been standing in a line so long he wasn't in a mood for further delay.

When the man in front of him reached the teller and pulled a gun, Trent's patience ran out.

"Clear out!" he cried.

The startled gunman didn't argue. He cleared out.

**It figures.**   During the 1980s, bank robberies in the U.S. increased. So banks *decreased* the number of armed guards.

Sound crazy?

Bank officials had an excuse. The sight of a guard with a pistol on his hip, they said, raised the likelihood for violence.

An unstated reason for the cutback was the payroll. Bankers took to heart a 1986 report by the FBI. According to the FBI's figures, the average bank heist netted $5,251. The cost in wages of a full-time guard was higher.

**Coffee break of the century.**   Workers knocking down an old building in Macon, Georgia, discovered a 200-foot tunnel. It led across the street to the wall enclosing the vault in the Citizens & Southern Bank. No one knows when the tunnel was dug, or why it was abandoned so close to its objective, or who dug it.

"You'd like to have somebody that industrious working for you," said a bank vice-president.

**Yawn stopper.**   His audience was nodding off as a candidate for office in Milwaukee County, Wisconsin, droned on about the money that park water-slides had brought in while he was parks director.

"We've more than paid for two of those water-slides, and we've got —"

His next words snapped everyone awake.

"You guys have got a bank robbery across the street," he said, pointing to the First Wisconsin National Bank. He had glimpsed two masked men running from the bank. They got away with several thousand dollars.

"Now look," the candidate said. "I promised to bring excitement to county government, but this is ridiculous."

**Let the good times roll.** "Have a pleasant day," the man said to Claudia Clandon, 75, as he cut through her backyard in Chattanooga after robbing the bank next door.

**Zzzzzz.** Worn out by three hours of effort trying to break through the walls of a bank vault, L. Y. Innjui of Nairobi, Kenya, lay down for a snooze. He was still asleep, perhaps dreaming of a wild and carefree life, when police clapped him in 'cuffs.

**Those were the days.** Malcolm Pitts was the high-living cashier at the People's Bank of Portsmouth in Richmond, Virginia, in 1905. A five-year sentence for slipping $800,000 of the bank's funds into his pocket didn't dampen his style. He rode to the penitentiary in a private railroad car accompanied by 12 friends and one sheriff.

**I just can't put my finger on it.**   A woman used her foot to rob the Standard Chartered Bank in Manama, Bahrain.

For several months Sari Haccera succeeded in beating the bank's system for helping its uneducated customers.

She doused her big toe in black ink and stepped on withdrawal slips, forging the thumbprints of folks who couldn't write their names.

She got $75,000 — and a three-month sentence.

**Try a little tenderness.**   A young aircraft mechanic, bent on getting rich quick, pulled a gun on a teller in a bank in Jersey City. She refused to give him anything but a flat no.

He seemed more shocked at the sight of her than by her answer. He bolted, but didn't stay free for long.

The teller knew his name and his address. She once dated him.

**Seemed like a good idea at the time.** A robber walked into the same Alabama bank he had robbed before. He wore a stocking mask again and held the same weapon.

Well, hello and —

An FBI agent just happened to be showing his photograph to tellers who had witnessed the first robbery.

— Gotcha!

"His timing was the pits," said a bank officer.

**Lemonaid.** In Maryland a man rubbed his face with lemon juice because he'd been told it would keep bank cameras from picking up his picture. It didn't work, and the police made him come clean.

# 5.
# Police Beat

**Your thoughts are not my thoughts, neither are your ways my ways.** In Philadelphia, a woman who sought to take the examination for police officer complained that all the test sites were in neighborhoods too dangerous to enter alone.

**Meet me in Fort Wayne.** You say you'd like to live in a place where folks are honest? Hustle over to Fort Wayne, Indiana.

Police there attempted to trap thieves by placing an expensive new TV set in an unlocked, parked car.

After a few weeks of watching from a van, the police gave up.

"People walked past the car, looked at the TV, opened the door, pushed the lock button down, closed the door, and walked on," a policeman said. "Nobody tried to take it."

69

**Snooty Louise.** In Hildesheim, West Germany, a female cop answered to the name of Louise and didn't mind being called a pig.

That's because she was one — a 220-pound wild boar.

Dressed in a snazzy harness, Louise was regularly used as a supersniffer. Her trainer, Werner Franke, maintained that Louise could outsniff any canine tracker.

"She can zero in on all known narcotics buried to a depth of four and a half feet," said Werner. "She can't be put off the scent by noises and other smells like dogs can.

"Further," he added, "pigs can sniff all day without rest and cover a lot of ground. It's their instinct. They are ideal for what we call large-area sniffing."

Purists in the Interior Ministry of Lower Saxony thought a pig was bad for the image of the force. They pressed for her retirement.

Instantly, pig lovers rose to her defense. Lower Saxony Premier Ernst Albrecht wrote a eulogy to her. Others called for "guard-pig units" to replace German shepherds.

So Louise's sizeable nose stayed on the job, and she received the title of *schuffelwildschwein,* or "sniffing wild boar."

She never hammed it up. She earned her 110 marks ($50) monthly. Most of it went for food.

"She did not take any old biscuit," said Franke. "Only the expensive Dutch ones with lots of chocolate coating or Danish butter cookies. I must have spoiled her."

**Pounds were grounds.** For safety's sake, the Washington, D.C., police placed a 195-pound limit on officers riding motor scooters. The next day nearly half the scooter patrol had to be grounded.

**Where, oh, where are you?** On April Fool's Day, Philadelphia police sent letters to hard-to-find former prisoners suspected of crimes since their release.

The letters told the ex-prisoners that the "Philadelphia Prison Reimbursement Fund," a made-up organization, owed them as much as $475 for their imprisonment.

The letter was mailed to 90 fugitives at their last known addresses and to their relatives and friends. Thirteen wanted men showed up at the Philadelphia Detention Center to pick up their cash and were immediately booked.

A detective said he got the idea from the police in Denver. They caught 67 fugitives the previous January by promising free football tickets.

**Catch-as-catch-can.** Two officers pursuing a fugitive on a beach in Swansea, Wales, shouted, "Follow that man!"

The operator of a mechanical excavator obliged. He scooped up the officers with his huge shovel and put the ten-ton machine into high gear. It went fast enough to overtake the breathless theft suspect. Then it sank in the soft sand. High tide covered it.

The police got their man, and the construction company got a repair bill of $7,200.

**Help wanted.** Rita Conrad of Perrine, Florida, wanted to become a policewoman. So she filled out an application. Her fingerprints revealed how badly the police wanted her, too. There were 11 bench warrants out on her.

**A poultry offense.**   Police in Fort Fairfield, Maine, got wind of a stray chicken roosting in a car on Main Street. The police arrested the fowl offender and read it its rights.

The chicken went into the record as "Cee Little" of Main Street. The charges: criminal mischief, criminal trespass, public indecency, resisting an officer, and littering.

"It started out as a joke and shouldn't have gone as far as it did," said the officer. "But in a town like Fort Fairfield [population 4,300], you have to do something to keep from going crazy."

The next morning, the four-pound bird was released into the custody of a chap who liked eggs.

**She didn't get ripped off.** A policewoman in New Orleans tore her trousers while chasing a teenage girl suspected in an auto theft. The policewoman filed suit against the girl's mother in small claims court for $31.86, the cost of the trousers.

To make amends for her daughter's conduct, the upset mother dropped $52 off at the court clerk's office.

"This is really terrific," said the happy policewoman. "You know, officers are always getting sued for harrassment when we're doing our jobs. Yet we have the same rights as any citizen. It's time we stand up and start using the laws to our own advantage."

**Now you see it, now you don't.** The new 300-pound safe in the Cochran, Georgia, police department was stolen while the officers were on night patrol.

**Police Academy.** In Manchester, England, an exercise to train policemen in riot control became too much like the real thing. Twenty officers were carted off to the hospital.

**Making it.** Benjamin Ward was appointed New York City's Police Commissioner 40 years after being named "police commissioner for a day," the prize for winning a citywide essay contest.

**His prize was a can of oil.** RMI-3 received New York City's "Cop of the Month" award in 1984.

RMI-3 was a $22,000 robot. It stood four feet tall, had six wheels, one arm, and weighed 230 pounds.

The robot earned its award for work during a shootout between police and two gunmen holed up in an apartment in Elmira, New York.

It shoved open a door, scanned the apartment, and was guided into the bathroom. Its video camera showed both gunmen out of action.

The pictures sent by RMI-3 assured the lawmen that the danger was ended.

Many police departments have robots now, but RMI-3 is believed to be the country's first to be named "Cop of the Month."

**And the winner is?** Everyone had fun at the policemen's annual ball in Meppen, West Germany.

There was one hitch. The door prizes were stolen. Not from the ball. *For* the ball.

An officer had robbed local stores for the prizes and forged receipts on a stolen typewriter.

**What every good cop should know.** You better be an "A" student in high school if you want to be a policeman in Málaga, Spain.

Some 3,000 people once took a test for 47 police cadet openings in the city. More than 2,000 flunked.

The test included such questions as:

In what year was Julio Acosta president of Costa Rica?

What do Alaskan fur seals eat?

What is the official currency of Madagascar?

Despite an uproar of protests, Police Commissioner Jacinto Mera defended the exam. The answers, he said, were in high school textbooks.

**What's my line?** The play was *The Hollow*, a murder mystery set in London, England.

During an evening performance in Miami, Florida, an urgent telephone call requested that a member of the audience, Police Captain Ron Finkiewicz, be notified of an emergency.

But how could they pass along the message to Finkiewicz without interrupting the play? No one connected with the theater knew him by sight.

The female lead solved the dilemma. She slipped the message into the dialogue.

"Oh, by the way, has Inspector Thorpe left yet?" she asked on stage.

"Yes, he has," another actor answered.

"Oh, that's a pity. I have a message for him from Captain Finkiewicz. His mother-in-law's home was broken into and she needs to get in touch with him right away."

Finkiewicz jumped up from his front-row seat. In the lobby he received details of the burglary. He hurried to investigate.

"It was so smooth it took a moment to sink in," he said later. "All of a sudden it dawned on me. The play was about a murder in London, not Poland. Why would there be someone with a Polish name like mine in it?"

# 6.
# Courtroom Capers

**Ooops.** Johnny Ray Burr, on trial for robbing a furniture store in Kansas City, Kansas, fired his lawyers and pleaded his own case.

Burr was doing pretty well — till the store owner identified him as the robber.

Burr jumped up and screamed, "Liar! I should have blown your [censored] head off!"

He caught himself, thought, and added quickly, "If I'd been the one that was there."

The jury convicted him in 20 minutes.

**They also drink a lot of coffee.** A judge in Belo Horizonte, Brazil, swore he would never accept a woman juror. He gave his reasons: Women shouldn't work outside the house, women are emotionally fragile, and the courtroom's toilet is dirty.

**Plea bargaining.** Burglar Marvin Mills of New York City was sentenced to seven years in the clink. Mills objected. Seven was his unlucky number. "Your Honor," he said. "Would you make it eight?"

It wasn't the kind of request the judge, David Katz, heard every day. He retired to his chambers and pondered for half an hour before granting Mills the extra year.

**With time off for good behavior?** A court in Bangkok, Thailand, sentenced Thanes Kham, a hotel cashier, to 865 years in prison for swiping $12,044.

The court later had a change of heart. It lowered his sentence to 576 years.

**What a rap.** While a judge in an Oklahoma County District Court was trying a case, someone stole his gavel.

**Oooh, when he got home.** Judge Leonard Finster, a police magistrate in Chicago, Illinois, ordered an offender who couldn't pay a ten-dollar fine locked up. When Mrs. Finster, seated near the bar, shouted, "That's an outrage!" he fined her $25.

**Five will get you ten.** Diego Fernandez, a car thief in Valparaíso, Chile, went to court seeking to have his bond lowered. Judge Joaquin Montt agreed, lowering bond in one auto theft charge from $5,000 to $2,500, and from $7,500 to $2,500 in another.

Fernandez seemed satisfied. Once in his cell again, he began to brood, then to curse, then to threaten. Jailers dragged him back to the courtroom.

Judge Montt asked what was wrong.

Fernandez swore some and retorted, "If you ever want to tell me anything, mail it to me."

"I won't have to mail you this," the judge said. "I'm finding you in contempt of court. One year in jail!"

"Why not make it five!" Fernandez shouted.

"All right, five," the judge agreed.

"Why not ten?"

"Ten years it is."

"Go on, raise the bonds to fifty thousand," Fernandez dared.

The judge did better. He raised the bonds to $100,000 and sent Fernandez to jail for ten years.

**Judge not.**  When some educated thieves in Mexico City learned the man they had robbed was a judge, they mailed back the money, $1,150, with an apology, "Pardon us. To err is human."

**Cool, man.**  A fleet-footed robbery suspect ran from a San Francisco courthouse with the police hard on his heels.

80

One of the officers, Murray Burton, cut past a nearby hotel pool.

"He went that way, officer!" cried a man in the pool.

Burton pulled up. He ordered the man, who wore only boxer shorts, out of the pool.

"He might have got away with it if he had escaped in the summertime," said Burton. "But the temperature was sixty degrees, and he was the only one in the pool."

**Book celler.** Robert Reari of Harare, Zimbabwe, was writing a book when he was convicted of robbery and impersonating an officer.

"It looks as if you'll have to finish your book in prison," said Justice Wilson Sandura. He gave Reari plenty of time — four and a half years.

Reari had titled his book, *Crime Does Not Pay*.

**Come clean.** Judges in Rochester, New York, started a new program of sentencing. Instead of being fined or jailed, nonviolent lawbreakers were made to do community service.

One man, convicted of drunken driving, had to clean the elephant cage at the zoo.

His service was a one-way success. He rode the bus to work, but the driver wouldn't let him on when he finished his smelly job. He had to walk home.

**He went ape.** Testifying against a drug dealer, an undercover police officer in Omaha, Nebraska, took the stand wearing a gorilla mask to hide his identity.

When the deputy police chief heard the officer was making a monkey of himself in court, he ordered him to find another disguise.

The following day the officer testified with a pillowcase over his head.

**Nothing could be finer than to be in Carolina.** A circuit court judge in Union, South Carolina, fined himself for being 15 minutes late to court. He got stuck in traffic during the 60-mile drive from his home in Lexington.

"I can't expect anyone else to be on time and then I show up late," he said.

He sentenced himself to ten days in jail or a one-dollar fine. He paid the fine.

**Show and tell.** Holly Puig wore only a turban and the American flag stapled in front when she answered a shoplifting charge. "I love my country," she told the judge. The judge dressed down the Syracuse woman and gave her 30 days in jail for contempt of court.

# 7.
# Behind Bars

**Shucks, ask me a hard one.**  The Law Enforcement Assistance Administration once spent $27,000 of the taxpayers' money to find out why prisoners want to escape from jail.

**Bingo!**  Gabriel Lopez didn't celebrate his 33rd birthday in the happiest of surroundings.

A cosmetics salesman, he was spending three years in prison at Punta Arenas, Chile, for passing $8,000 in bad checks.

But wait.

As a birthday present, a cellmate gave him a lottery card for the Chilean soccer championship series. Lopez filled it out, guessing correctly the results of all 13 games. He won $170,000.

According to the law in Chile, persons imprisoned for passing bad checks can be set free if they pay their debts.

For Lopez, it had been a happy birthday after all.

**Investing in his future.** Prisoners on Rikers Island in New York City took a class in the stock market. One day the teacher passed around a stock certificate.

An inmate accused of forgery studied it a little too long. When he asked about the kind of ink and paper used to print it, a guard yanked it away.

**Sink your teeth into this one.** Rafael Reyes, 62, of Rio Cuarto, Argentina, went back to jail because he couldn't chew.

Shortly after his imprisonment, he had to have his teeth pulled for health reasons. The prison dentist promised him a set of false teeth. When he was released, however, his gums were still naked.

Reyes told a judge in Pergamino he was ill because he couldn't gum his food fine enough to digest. His illness kept him from getting a job to pay for new choppers.

The judge directed the prison dentist to finish the job.

Said His Honor, "Every man has a right to bite," or words to that effect.

**Reha*bill*itation.** Phony $100 bills circulating in Richmond, Virginia, drew an investigation by Secret Service agents. The bills were traced to crafty cons working in a print shop — at the Virginia State Penitentiary.

**He should have had it delivered.**   Giuseppe Russo, a warden in Gissi, Italy, was sentenced to seven months in his own jail for freeloading.

Once a week he let his prisoners take him out for a pizza. After they had stuffed themselves, he allowed them to go home and sleep it off.

Police learned of his pizza night when a prisoner's mother complained her son had raised a ruckus in the living room.

**Battery up!**   A power failure plunged the Idaho State Penitentiary into pitch-blackness. Quick-witted officials encircled the prison with cars and used their headlights to prevent escapes.

**It's easy to be critical, but hard to be correct.** Klaus Kramer of Dortmund, West Germany, spent two years in jail because of his nose.

Kramer had been sentenced to six years mainly because of photographs of a huge-nosed man sticking up a bank, and the testimony of witnesses.

A court-appointed schnoz expert said uh-uh. Kramer's nose was definitely not the one snapped by the bank's automatic camera.

Kramer was released, and for each day in jail he received four dollars.

**Soft cell.** In 1985, the opening of the new El Dorado County jail in California had to be delayed. The cell doors didn't lock.

**Return to sender.** The customer relations boss at a mail-order house was surprised to get back an order of Special Forces-type boots and a lined poncho.

The merchandise had been shipped to a Richard Seward at an address that turned out to be the Mississippi State Prison. Seems prison officials, who check all packages, didn't want Seward or any other inmate preparing for a long hike.

**Hard to stomach.** Smoking can be bad for your health and happiness, especially if you have to cough up cash for a pack of cigarettes as Oscar Heath did.

On his first day in the Grand Traverse County jail in Traverse City, Michigan, he inquired if smokes were to be had.

The guards said sure. But he'd have to come up with a dollar a pack.

Heath obliged, nearly. He coughed up a ten-dollar bill, which he had wrapped in a plastic bag and gulped down earlier.

He tried again and pulled a $20 bill from his mouth.

Anyone who has ever kept money in his stomach can understand Heath's problem. It's so hard to find the right change.

Under prison rules, inmates' money had to be kept by prison officials, and not in stomachs. Heath was charged with possessing illegal goods.

He was already serving sentences for grand larceny and for shoplifting a can of chocolate syrup.

**Dialing out.**   Inmates in the Orange County jail in California used the jail telephones to shorten their sentences.

Pretending to be state correctional officials, they spoke to judges and won early releases.

**Bare walls do not a prison make.**   Prisoners in England's Haverigg Prison are a quick-tempered lot.

Make that hot-tempered.

They set a fire that gutted the kitchen, clothing

exchange store, education departments, and several wings. Sixteen men escaped during the rioting.

What started it all?

An unbearable injustice.

The prisoners were told to remove pinups from freshly painted walls.

# 8.
# Aw-a-a-ay We Go!

**Whistle while you work.** Prisoners in Israel's Ramallah prison were hours away from breaking out.

They never made it.

Blame their singing. It sounded like a flock of birds chirping off-key.

The warden, Muphid Abas, grew curious. He sneaked close and spied the jailbirds chipping a hole in a cell wall with metal slabs from their beds. The noise of the work was drowned out by the noisier songfest.

Abas put an end to both chipping and chirping.

**The hole-in-the-wall gang.** In Wisconsin the warden of the Dane County jail had all posters taken down from cell walls and ceilings after three inmates escaped through a hole covered by a pinup.

**Dead giveaway.**  Hilary Sherman shipped out of a Vancouver Island prison in a coffin.

The coffin was a prop in the play *Dracula,* staged by fellow convicts. After the applause, Sherman stole the coffin, roped it to a homemade catamaran, and paddled his way to freedom.

**It suited him.**  An inmate with an eye for the correct traveling clothes made it look easy. He sawed the bars in the showers of the Florida State prison, slipped through a gate that led to the front gate, and strolled out.

He wore a coat and a hat and had painted his prison pants and shirt brown to resemble a guard's uniform.

**Leave well enough alone.** Sam Ryan of Winnipeg, Canada, was locked up for forging a $600 check. He escaped, and it was three days before anyone noticed he was missing.

He might be free today except for wanting what was his. He returned to the city jail to pick up his wallet, which had been confiscated when he was arrested.

**Stop payment!** Michigan officials discovered that 92 escaped prisoners were receiving welfare checks.

**The truth will set you free.** Police helped robbers break *out* of a tavern in Reno, Nevada.

Two young women had hidden in a storeroom at closing time. All went well until they tried to leave with their loot. The place was rigged like Fort Knox to prevent illegal entries — and exits. They had to telephone for help.

**Personal best.** Antonio D'Allessio paid for the damages he caused while busting out of jail in Milan, Italy.

D'Allessio and another prisoner smashed through the ceiling and roof on their route to freedom. Later D'Allessio telephoned a prison official to find out the amount of the damages. It was more than $500. He sent his check.

That wasn't the first time D'Allessio had made

good. He had inherited "a lot of money," according to his attorney, while in a lockup near Novara. He did about $300 in damages there during an unsuccessful breakout attempt. He had his attorney send a check to cover the cost of the repairs.

After the Milan escape, D'Allessio was recaptured and shifted to a top security prison.

**Bar none.** In 1984, four prisoners escaped from a jail in Oristano, Sardinia. Their method was a textbook example of old-fashioned know-how.

The foursome cut through the bars of their cell with a file that a relative had delivered in a loaf of bread. Then they dropped to the ground by means of a knotted bed sheet.

The red-faced guards refused comment.

**Nice try.** John Scott was the only man to break out of Alcatraz and live to tell of it.

In 1984, twenty-two years later, marathon swimmers Dave Horning and Randy Williams celebrated the anniversary of Scott's feat. They re-created his swim across the two-and-one-half miles of icy, shark-filled water from Alcatraz Island to San Francisco.

Both men utterly exhausted themselves, and Williams was treated for hypothermia.

Even so, they were more successful than Scott, who hadn't been able to make good his escape. The cops had welcomed him with open handcuffs as he staggered ashore.

**Hey, pinhead.** Alf Reiner wriggled through a five-inch-wide window in his holding cell in Edmonton, Canada.

"You've got to see the guy's head to believe it," said a corrections officer. "The escape was the talk of the prison, especially how stupid he was to get caught less than two hours later."

**Hi ho, hi ho, it's off to jail we go, again.** Ben Garland and Willie Winslow were a couple of long-termers at a state prison in Huntsville, Texas. While unloading furniture in the woodshop, they got this great idea. Use the trailer-truck they were unloading to escape.

The truck drove off with them in back. Fifteen miles down the road it stopped — inside another unit of the state prison system.

**Power of the press.** Guards at the main jail in Oslo, Norway, didn't know of a prisoner's escape until a newspaper informed them.

Acting on a tip, a reporter for *Verdens Gang,* Norway's biggest daily, called the jail and said Erik Larsen had cut the bars of his cell window and slid to freedom down a rope.

The reporter met with disbelief until a guard looked into Larsen's cell.

"We consider the man to be dangerous," said Oslo's police chief, Magnar Aukrust.

**All's fare . . .**   Manfred Bach skipped out of a minimum security prison in Stillwater, Minnesota, on Christmas Eve. He waved down a taxi and had the cabbie drive him 110 miles to his mother's house.

Lacking the Christmas spirit of giving, Bach refused to tip the cabbie. He also refused to pay the $125 fare.

The cabbie tipped the police. Bach's return trip was made in a squad car.

**Genius at work.**   Kyle Hogan strolled into a Savannah police station. He had a little problem. He'd lost his identification card. Could anyone tell him how to replace it?

Good question, wrong place.

The police checked his identity with the National Crime Information Center, which listed him as an escapee from a Georgia prison.

He received a replacement identification card — in prison.

# 9.
# Alibi Ikes

**Pipe dream.** Two men who broke into a church near Frankfort, Indiana, told police they only wanted to play the organ.

**A loaf of bread, a jug of wine?** Four cons in a Wyoming state prison swore to a judge that what they'd dug under the floor of their cellblock wasn't a tunnel but a wine cellar.

**That certain feeling.** An ex-policeman of Carlow, Ireland, blamed his burglaries on eating too many doughnuts. The doughnuts brought on ups and downs in his blood-sugar levels, leading to "wicky-wacky" behavior, he claimed.

The judge saw the hole in his story and sentenced him to seven to fifteen years.

**That's off (not over) the wall.** While awaiting sentencing on a burglary charge, Harmon Tully escaped over the wall of a jail in San Francisco. Recaptured, he told the judge: "I was playing pole vault and I got too close to the wall and fell over. When I regained my senses, I ran around trying to find my way back in. I got lost. The next thing I knew I was in Los Angeles."

**What'd he say?** A Rhode Island man driving a stolen car was pulled over by a police officer. "Please don't arrest me," pleaded the car thief. "I stole it to go to court to answer a burglary charge."

**Well, mow me down.** A Washington man was fined $65 for shooting his lawnmower with a .357 caliber magnum pistol. He told the judge that he got angry when it wouldn't start, and it still won't.

**A flue-ky story.** A youth who got stuck in the chimney of a country club outside St. Louis said he was only trying to make a delivery.

**Nailed.** Sandy Miller, a manicurist from Trenton, New Jersey, said she had become a millionaire through meditation.

The jury said her forefinger was responsible and found her guilty of grand theft.

Miller had hit upon a glitch in her bank's computer program. Regularly she punched in hefty sums on the automatic teller without depositing a cent.

**Cry panic.** A New City attorney, arrested for leaping over a subway turnstile, claimed he was trying to make it to the church on time for his wedding.

**Fiddling with the truth.** Jarvis Colby, an American violin maker living in France, insisted he didn't steal a helicopter. "I was forced at gunpoint to fly that chopper," he said. "After I was freed, I didn't return it because I didn't want to miss dinner."

**The savings and loan diet.** A car salesman on trial for bank robbery in Cleveland claimed he went to a hypnotist in an effort to lose weight, and the hypnotist left him with an overpowering urge to rob a bank.

**Daddy Ghostbucks.** Cynthia Brandon of Denver said her father's ghost persuaded her to steal $50,000 from her former boss. The judge dismissed the case against the ghost but gave Brandon 20 years.

# 10.
# For the Record

**Open-door policy.** After being burglarized 36 times in three years, Jim Barton, a 72-year-old news vendor of Bethnal Green, England, stopped locking his room. He had nothing left worth stealing.

**The awful truth.** In 1985, Katie Smith, a London pickpocket, was picked up by the bobbies for the 31st time. During a life of crime that dated back to 1926, the frail 75-year-old widow had spent 20 years in prison.

"My fingers are not as good as they used to be," Katie wheezed. "I'm retiring."

**I smell a rat.** Do crooks have a special air about them?

Before you turn up your nose at that idea, pay attention. Researchers at Leeds University in England are into "odorprints."

They're bottling the scent from the bodies of volunteers.

"Folks at the hospital tend to look at me a bit strangely," admits one of the researchers, Barbara Sommerville.

She claims everyone has an individual odor, criminals included. The main problem is finding a sensitive, reliable smell-detector.

Under consideration is the use of antennas of mosquitoes and flies. The little buggers are really good smellers.

Even if the odorprints are developed, the way to beat the new style of law and odor is foreseen.

The bad guys will drench themselves with aftershave lotions, colognes, and deodorants.

"England may someday have the sweetest-smelling criminals the world has ever sniffed," said Sommervile.

**Tale of the tape.** Police asked Maurice C. Snow to describe the man who had bound, gagged, and robbed him.

"Of course," agreed Snow, a shopkeeper in Worcester, Massachusetts, who provided this portrait:

The robber was 5 foot 10 and weighed between 165 and 170 pounds. His neck was 14½ inches and his sleeve 25½ inches. He had a 39-inch chest, a 34-inch waist, and 41-inch hips.

The description, said the police, was the most detailed they'd ever got from a victim.

And why not? Before he was robbed of a camera, a watch, and $24, Snow had measured the man for a suit.

**They like it like that.**   The custom of taking off one's shoes before entering a home is so strong in Korea that even burglars do so before breaking in.

**Fighting for dollars.**   Is a black eye worth it? For centuries the question floated from person to person without a definite opinion.

In 1988, the British government nailed down the answer.

A genuine shiner is worth $168.

The sum is part of the price list of punches the Home Office gave out to judges. Now toughs must pay folks they beat up on.

A slight puffing from a grazing swing brings a mere $84. One eye closed and blackened earns you $168. Really get worked over — limp out of the hospital with your head in a cast, say — and you can look forward to a soothing $2,940.

**Ho, ho, ho.**   Some of the world's best pickpockets are trained at "The School of Ten Bells" in Bogotá, Colombia. The tuition is more than $3,000, and the final exam is a ding-a-ling.

A mannequin is dressed in a three-piece suit with sleighbells hung on the ten pockets. To graduate, the student has to empty the pockets without raising a tinkle.

**A penny saved.**   In 1984, Hope Denner of Bend, Oregon, paid the heaviest fine in the history of the state.

The sum, $505, was for eluding police. To pay it, she saved her pennies for five years.

Two friends helped her carry 1,010 rolls of pennies — 455.6 pounds — to the courthouse, and lay them on the desk of the county clerk.

He said Denner was 46 cents shy.

**Going one better.** Artist Brett Wynn of West Palm Beach, Florida, presented the police with a signed, framed 24-by-30-inch oil painting of the man who ripped off his $1,000 gold neckchain.

**Go fight city hall.** An 80-year-old man tried to hold up a post office in downtown Jacksonville, Florida.

"You're out of luck," said a clerk. "The counters aren't open yet."

The man knew better than to reason with a government employee. He lowered his head forlornly and tottered away.

**Now they tell us.** A sign in a Tokyo hotel room was widely reprinted in the United States.

IS FORBIDDEN TO STEAL TOWELS, PLEASE.
IF YOU ARE NOT PERSON TO DO SUCH
PLEASE DO NOT READ NOTICE.

**Sorry, wrong number.** In 1981, teenager Barry Donaldson hopped on his motorcycle and set off for a Sunday spin in Parma, Ohio.

Police stopped him for changing lanes without signaling.

The next thing he knew, his bike was being towed away. He was taken to the police station and charged with possession of stolen property.

Ten days later, a patient detective proved Donaldson's motorcycle was not stolen. A manufacturer's error was at fault.

In 1976 the same serial number had been stamped on the frame of two bikes at the Kawasaki factory. Both were model KZ-900, and they had the same features and color.

"A one-in-a-million chance," said the detective. "In fact, the odds are probably even greater than that."

One of the motorcycles was stolen in 1977. The other wound up in a cycle shop in Milan, Ohio. Donaldson bought it fourth-hand for $1,700, two weeks before his arrest.

His innocence was established because the two bikes had different engine serial numbers.

Bad news came with the good. He had to pay $70 in storage fees to get the motorcycle back.

**Lettuce now praise the refrigerator.** To help the homeowner foil robbers, a company in Torrance, California, introduced a $15 head of lettuce made of vinyl. Inside was a jar to hold cash and other valuables.

"We got the idea after someone mentioned a burglary where everything was cleaned out but the refrigerator," said Gary Northrop, the sales manager.

**The light that failed.** The government of Taiwan banned video game arcades. A spokesman said some children had become juvenile delinquents, "stealing, robbing, and fighting" after they got hooked on the games.

**In England you can see trees with proper pedigrees.** Trees planted in a new industrial park in Birmingham, England, were selected for their slender trunks. City planners didn't want muggers to hide behind them.

**Homeowners insurance.** Eighty-year-old Arnold Clinton of New Orleans had a hunch his home would be robbed while he was on vacation.

So before leaving, the retired seaman left money, a bottle of whiskey, and a note on the kitchen table. The note read:

> To the Burglar:
> Here is 51 dollars and about 30 or 40 dollars in change. Also a bottle of whiskey. All yours. There is no need to ransack the house looking for more money as it's all here. Don't be a jerk and steal anything. Be honest.

Upon his return, Clinton discovered the thief had followed instructions. He took the money and left the whiskey and everything else in the house untouched.

**High risk.** A convicted counterfeiter, now a businessman in Fort Worth, Texas, discussed the perils of his former profession.

"Counterfeiting tens and twenties isn't worth the effort and the risks," he said. "You have to keep moving from one store to another. This increases the danger because you are forced to deal with people you can't trust."

**Body works.** If Air Force Major Fred Murphy has the same luck in the air as he does on the ground, he may be America's next ace.

He was shot at close range by a robber. The bullet bounced off his chest.

Murphy, who was stationed at Langley Air Force Base in Virginia, was held up by two men at the automatic teller of the Virginia National Bank. He gave them his money, but one of them pulled the trigger just the same.

The bullet left a bruise on his chest and burns on his coat. When Murphy just stood there, the robbers fled.

Did Murphy chase them?

"Are you crazy?" he said.

**Modern job.** Luis Ortez of Miami, Florida, was told to wait in a room in headquarters for questioning in connection with a barroom brawl.

He waited patiently.

Saturday came and went. So did Sunday and Monday.

People asked, "What are you doing here?"

"I'm waiting for Detective Rodriguez," he replied.

He was told to stay where he was.

Tuesday passed. He'd had nothing to eat or drink. When he had to use the bathroom, he requested permission.

Wednesday he inquired if Detective Rodriguez was ever going to question him.

That's when someone thought to ask how long he'd been waiting.

*How long?*

Turned out Ortez had not been charged. An officer had been ordered to drive him home on Saturday. The officer went to the wrong room. Someone else got the ride.

For his five-day wait, Ortez accepted a $2,500 settlement from the city.

**I'll grab the dough, Fred, you do the driving.** By 1982, the economy in England had fallen so low that some criminals couldn't afford a getaway car.

A couple of hoods held up a North London post office and got $4,000. Then they jumped on a bicycle. One pedaled like mad while the other sat on the handlebars and waved a sawed-off shotgun.

**Surprise.**  To thwart purse-snatchers, an inventor in Detroit designed a handbag that falls apart if tugged.

**Never drink alone.**  Roland Weeks, an Irish safe-cracker, needed a drink to steady his nerves.

One drink led to another. . . .

A security guard in a Dublin office building found him snoring by the safe, his burglar's tools strewn over the floor, a half-empty bottle of wine by his chair.

**Because all books should have a happy ending.**  A Kansas man and woman met when he commandeered her car at pistolpoint with the police hot on his heels. The couple announced plans to marry while he served a one- to five-year sentence for burglary.

## Solution to
## The Case of the
## Two-Headed Toothbrush

Bugs knew nothing about coin laundry machines. So he simply repeated what Melvin told Encyclopedia.

Melvin, who was washing clothes, said, "I had the lid of the machine raised and was pushing the laundry down inside it with both hands. . . ."

Bugs told the same story. However, he changed one fact so it wouldn't seem as if he were just mouthing Melvin's account.

Bugs said he was *drying* clothes.

That was his mistake!

Encyclopedia whispered into his ear, "You lift the *lid* and push clothes *down* only in a washing machine. A dryer doesn't have a lid on top. It has a door in the side."

Bugs couldn't have dried his clothes in a washing machine!

# About the Author

Donald J. Sobol was born in New York City and attended Oberlin College in Oberlin, Ohio. After serving with the U.S. Army Combat Engineers in the Pacific Theater during World War II, he worked on the editorial staffs of the *New York Sun* and the *Long Island Daily Press*.

A writer for more than twenty-five years, he has written sixty books. He now lives in Miami, Florida, with his wife, Rose Sobol, and enjoys scuba diving and restoring antique cars.